Au

MICHELLE OBAMA: A FEMININE LEADERSHIP

Strategies for Female Leadership without Resorting to Male Skills

Published by UNIBOOKS

UNIBOOKS
DIGITAL PUBLISHER

1

TABLE OF CONTENTS

6. Leading in Style: Public Image and Popular Culture

INTRODUCTION

Women and Leadership: A Natural Fit

Women are not new to leadership. Women have been leading for thousands of years, primarily within the nucleus of the family. The exceptional interpersonal skills and intuition that women tend to have puts them in a position to excel at this role. Yet in the fronts of business and politics, women are relative newcomers, holding only 4.6 percent of CEO positions in Fortune 500 companies and 19 positions as elected presidents and prime ministers worldwide.

In a world where women are severely underrepresented in prominent leadership positions, people are beginning to realize that women may be more naturally inclined towards leadership than men. This book will examine a woman who exemplifies many of the best qualities of female leaders of our time. As the First Lady of the United States of America, she is in a position of power, but also in a position in which her leadership is questioned because her husband is *the* leader of the entire country. We will look at the ways in which she uses her natural leadership qualities to her full advantage to take on her own initiatives and truly affect positive change.

Before we delve into what makes Michelle Obama an exceptional leader, let's take a look at the qualities that women most often exhibit that gives them the potential to become amazing leaders.

First, women are known for possessing strong instincts and a much higher level of emotional intelligence than men. They are statistically better at networking and cultivating interpersonal relationships than men, which is an invaluable skill in any business or political environment.

In contrast to the competitive, ladder-climbing mentality often ascribed to male business successes, women are more often inclined to stick together and protect one another on that same climb. Far from holding them back, this gives women a huge advantage when it comes to project management and team leadership.

Finally, women are givers. Female leaders are characteristically just as concerned about lifting up whole communities and organizations as they are with climbing to success. Think about it: competitive qualities are useless to a leader if they cannot be used to collaborate and push the entire community or organization forward. By being concerned with all parts of the whole, female leaders find success in effectively leading organizations without leaving anyone behind and causing inefficiencies.

A 2011 Forbes article metaphorically describes women's approach to leadership in business and politics as an "immigrant mindset." In the same way that an immigrant acts in a new country or environment, women are resourceful, success-driven and ready to react to a constantly changing environment. Michelle Obama was born into a changing world in terms of attitudes towards female leadership and discrimination towards black Americans. Stubborn and opinionated, yet compassionate and driven, she serves as an excellent example from which we can learn the most effective leadership skills.

1. LEADING IN LIFE FROM AN EARLY AGE

1.1 A Heavy Burden: Family History

Michelle Obama's story follows the same thread as that of many African-Americans living in the United States. Her great-great grandmother, Melvinia Shields, was a slave in Clayton County, Georgia. Her great-great grandfather on her father's side, Jim Robinson, was also a slave in South Carolina. As is characteristic of so many US families, the family was multiracial, with Michelle's ancestors being from Ireland and many other European countries.

1.2 African-American Female, and Discriminated Against: Early Life

Born Michelle LaVaughn Robinson on January 17, 1964, Michelle describes her childhood as having taken place in a "conventional home" by explaining that this meant "the mother at home, the father works, you have dinner around the table." Her brother, Craig, was two years older than her, and the two siblings were raised primarily by their mother. Michelle and Craig shared a part of the family's living room as a sleeping space, which was separated from the rest of the room by a sheet.

Throughout her childhood, Michelle was surrounded by a network of family and extended relatives in the close community of Chicago's South Shore neighborhood. There is no doubt that her relationships with the strong female leaders throughout her life influenced the woman she has become.

Interestingly, her childhood has been described as a classic American story, while her then-to-be future husband Barack's is far from typical. She may not have faced any horrific stories of prejudice or discrimination, but her day to day experiences reflected a high level of casual racism and sexism.

In Peter Slevin's recent biography of Michelle, titled *Michelle Obama: A Life*, he tells how, "The message was rooted in a paradox that required elders to hold two seemingly contradictory ideas in mind simultaneously. One was the fact that the playing field was tilted away from their children because of their race and class. The other was the conviction that a combination of love, support, perseverance, and upright living could win out."

In Michelle's case, she was never taught that her gender put her at a disadvantage, yet she was reminded of it all the time in encounters throughout her childhood. In an anecdote, Michelle remembers that peers and adults in school often talked to her brother first, ignoring her when the two were together, both because she was younger and because she was female.

1.3 Leadership as a Female in the Robinson Family

The female members of Michelle's family were important role models in her life as examples of powerful stubbornness and strongly opinionated women. Michelle did not stray in terms of stubbornness: she was not an easy child. Slevin's biography highlights her cursing habit, and tells the anecdote of a camp experience she had when "at a city-run camp [on the shores of Lake Michigan], 10-year-old Michelle missed out on the best camper award because of her salty tongue."

Michelle's mother, Marian Robinson, remembered "she always had her own opinions about things and she didn't hesitate to say so, because we allowed it." Slevin continues that "LaVaughn Robinson, Michelle's paternal grandmother, told a coworker that Michelle was 'hardheaded and needed a spanking from time to time, but that she and Craig were good kids."

As her father suffered from multiple sclerosis, Michelle learned emotional strength from her mother, grandmothers, and other women her close community. Despite having a debilitating disease, her father commuted into the city every single day for his job as a pump worker at a water filtration plant. She recalls watching him get ready for work with difficulty, and seeing him leave for his job with two canes. Even with her sadness and concern for her father, she gained emotional strength from seeing him overcome these challenges so early in life.

1.4 Stubbornness, Strong Opinions, and Solid Leadership: Cultivate these Qualities in your Search for Success

You may have been born into a "conventional" tight-knit, strong-willed family like that of Michelle Obama's childhood. Or you may not have. Regardless of your background, let's consider ways that you can strengthen these qualities within yourself, which ultimately led to Michelle's leadership strength.

First, Michelle's stubborn quality, much like many other leaders, was not always appreciated in her early childhood. Ask yourself: what are the beliefs that you stand firmly behind? Do you ever waiver when others question what is important to you?

Second, recognize the importance of strong opinions. Michelle's parents were not free-for-all hands-off parents who let her do everything. They allowed their daughter to have her strong opinions, and cultivated an environment where it was ok to disagree. However, they let her know when she had crossed the line. As a female leader in today's business world, women must stand behind their opinions and not apologize for standing by what they think.

Finally, perhaps one of the most characteristically female leadership qualities that was underlined throughout Michelle's childhood was the importance of a solid family base. Women leaders throughout history have been masters of ensuring that solid family base. As we will see in later chapters, Michelle's attitude towards her career and her husband's political career comes from an attitude of family first--she gains strength from her family's wellbeing and support, and also uses it as an indicator of whether to take on new projects.

In the same way that female leaders should unapologetically stand behind their opinions and values, they should not have to apologize for prioritizing their family, if that is in fact a priority for them. As Michelle Obama demonstrates, her family is both one of her biggest motivators and her biggest boons to success in leadership.

2. EXCELLENCE IN EDUCATION

Michelle's education resulted as much from her success as from the challenges she faced emotionally and socially and the ways they fueled her fortitude. She held leadership roles throughout her high school career, but what would prove to serve her in the future was the way she confronted the harsh discrimination and negativity that she was faced with, both for being a woman and for her confidence in standing up against discrimination towards African-Americans.

For Michelle, leadership in college meant proving her worth at Princeton University and making it clear that she was meant to be there. Neither of her parents had attended university, and she paved her way as a first-generation college student.

Education was marked as a target in Michelle's life, and her ability to stubbornly set her sights on that goal allowed her to excel. Her experience in higher education serves as an excellent example of the goal-orientedness and focus that is so characteristic of successful female leaders.

2.1 Academic Excellence at the Whitney M. Young High School

There was no doubt about it: Michelle was a highly intelligent student. She and her brother both skipped the second grade, and by sixth grade she was taking classes in her school's gifted program, learning French, and taking accelerated courses in biology.

Despite the three-hour round-trip commute every day to the Whitney M. Young Magnet High School, Michelle took full advantage of her acceptance to this competitive institution. She showed signs of leadership in her performance: She was the treasurer of her student government, and graduated second in her class.

2.2 Gaining Emotional Strength

Despite being on the honor roll for her entire time in high school and graduating as salutatorian, Michelle's four years at the Whitney Young School were far from easy.

She dealt with classic high school challenges and insecurities. "I was afraid of not knowing the answer in class and looking stupid, or worried about what some boy thought of me, or wondering whether the other girls liked my clothes or hair," recalls Michelle in an interview.

Other thoughts were less self-conscious and more reflective of the difficulties she faced as an African-American female in her competitive high school environment. Michelle remembers "angsting about some offhand comment someone made to me in the lunchroom." She also recalls that some teachers at the school told her that she was "setting my sights too high" when she aimed to be accepted to Princeton University.

In spite of all the fear, doubt, and negativity that surrounded her, Michelle ultimately strengthened her sense of self during those tumultuous years of high school. Looking back now, she has said that she "used that negativity to fuel me, to keep me going." And she would need that fuel for the mounting challenges that she would face as a student at Princeton.

2.3 Challenges of a First-Generation College Student

Despite the many doubts, criticisms, and negative comments about how she wasn't made for a place like Princeton, Michelle was stronger than ever and ready for the challenges of college life. She says of some high school teachers: "They told me I was never going to get into a school like Princeton. I still hear that doubt ringing in my head."

Moving away from her familiar Chicago suburb to go to a wealthy, conservative, primarily white University was a new kind of challenge. White students at the school were unbelievably insensitive at times, and acted as if they had never seen African-American classmates; in fact, some of them never had.

After sailing through high school academically, Michelle was surprised by incredibly challenging classes, which led to a C during her first semester. What set her apart from many who were surprised by the challenging workload and material of Princeton was her characteristic stubbornness and will to succeed. When a professor commented "You're not the hottest thing I've seen coming out of the gate" she found herself even more determined to succeed. "I decided I was going to do everything in my power to make that man regret those words...I knew that it was my responsibility to show my professor how wrong he was about me." Finally, when she applied to Harvard Law School, he confirmed that Michelle had proven him wrong: he offered to write an extra letter of recommendation.

Michelle successfully graduated from Princeton in 1985 with a B.A. in Sociology, and countless contributions to the racial consciousness of the students and faculty of the university. She is reported as saying that she never stopped feeling like an outsider throughout her four years at Princeton. Her dedication to racial equality was far from finished as she continued her educational career at Harvard Law School.

In 1988, at Harvard, Michelle wrote a 3,000 word article in a campus newsletter calling for more diversity in Harvard's faculty. She reported that "The faculty's decision to distrust and ignore non-traditional qualities in choosing and tenuring law professors merely reinforces racist and sexist stereotypes."

Her work at Harvard Law was primarily focused on race, and less specifically on gender equality. What many overlook, though, is that Michelle made use of characteristically female leadership strategies to her advantage. "Michelle always, everything she wrote, the things she was involved in, the things that she thought about, were in effect reflections on race and gender," said one of her professors at the time.

2.4 Confronting Challenges of Personal Discrimination: Strategies to Overcome Obstacles in Becoming a Strong Leader

Michelle's experience in education was full of challenges and obstacles to her success. She faced doubt, uncertainty, fear and discrimination. But let's focus on the four most important lessons from this time in her life and how she learned to apply them for later leadership success.

The first quality that characterized this period in Michelle's life was her goal-orientedness. Michelle's ability to focus on the things that were most important in her life at the time: success in education and being involved in initiatives for racial and gender equality. As she got older, Michelle's focus on these goals only became stronger, and made it easier for her to brush off discriminatory comments or emotional struggles.

Second, Michelle's tendency to take advantage of opportunities that presented themselves was critical to her success.

Third, Michelle drew from her personal experiences and found empathy within herself to gain passion for the causes she cared about. As we will see in later chapters, education has been a critical part of many of

Michelle's initiatives as first lady. She uses her personal experiences and her sense of empathy to fuel her passion for these causes.

Finally, perhaps the most important quality of the future first lady was her bravery and overcoming of fear. Despite her tough, opinionated appearance, Michelle recalls herself as being "tangled up in fears and doubts that were entirely of my own creation." Looking back on this time of her life, she reflects that she would tell herself "Stop being so afraid!" As she grew up and continued her education, Michelle learned to channel this fear and convert it into the qualities that would make her such a powerful lawyer, and later First Lady: determination and passion.

3. CONFIDENCE AFTER COLLEGE AND EARLY LAW CAREER

3.1 Preparing for life after law school: Leading the Way after Harvard

By the time Michelle attended Harvard Law, gone was the uncertainty of her place in the academic world. Michelle was leading significant changes at the University, including initiatives involving hiring. While in law school, Michelle had held a job at Harvard Legal Aid Bureau, in which she worked to help local residents seeking legal advice and representation, but unable to afford professional assistance. During this job, Michelle gained important experience that would later help her when applying for competitive jobs after she graduated from Harvard.

3.2 Meeting Barack: Sidley Austin Law Firm

Following law school, Michelle accepted a job as an associate attorney at Sidley & Austin in Chicago, focusing on intellectual property rights and marketing with clients that included AT&T. The early success and six-figure salary gave her continued confidence in her career and abilities, as well as helped to pay off her significant student debt.

Although it didn't quite fit with her driving passion to serve her community, this job was a critical turning point in Michelle's life: it was where she met Barack.

In 1989, Michelle was assigned to be Barack's advisor during his summer internship at the law firm. Hesitant initially because of her desire to uphold her professional values and because of her value for her career, she soon gave in and fell in love with the young president-to-be.

Michelle's mother later revealed that she was concerned about the relationship early on. When commenting about him being biracial she said, "That didn't concern me as much as had he been completely white, and I guess that I worry about races mixing because of the difficulty, not so much for prejudice or anything. It's just very hard." Michelle's mother had a certain amount of support for the couple though, as she allowed them to live upstairs from her while for a period while Barack was studying for the Illinois Bar exam.

After dating for two years, Michelle and Barack married at the Trinity United Church of Christ on October 3, 1992, and began a partnership that would become the ultimate leadership duo.

3.3 Leading Roles in the Public Sector

1991 began with two life-shifting shocks for Michelle. Her father and a friend both died in the same year, pushing her to zero in on what was most important to her.

Despite the fact that it meant a significant pay cut compared to her law firm salary, Michelle followed her intuition and sought a job in the public sector to follow her passion of serving the community. In 1991, she accepted a job as assistant to the Mayor of the City of Chicago. For a year, she worked as a liaison between the city and new businesses.

Following her job as the Mayor's assistant, she worked as Assistant Commissioner of Planning and Development for the City of Chicago. In 1993, she became the Executive Director in the Chicago Office of Public Allies, a role in which she helped young adults learn skills to aid them in seeking public sector careers in the future.

Even when she left the public sector for jobs at the University of Chicago, Michelle continued to serve the community and search for ways to help the underprivileged population. In 1996, she started as Assistant Dean of Student Services at the University of Chicago and simultaneously developed the university's first community service program.

In 2002, Michelle worked for the University of Chicago Hospitals as Executive Director of Community Relations and External Affairs. In 2005, she took on the position of Vice President for Community and External Affairs at the University of Chicago Medical Center. During this time, Michelle also occupied the prestigious position of board member of the Chicago Council on Global Affairs.

It was only shortly before Barack's presidential inauguration in 2007 that Michelle completely left her then part-time position at the University of Chicago Medical center to dedicate herself completely to her family and her husband's campaign.

3.4 Concerned with all parts of the Whole: Female Leadership for Community Betterment

In this chapter, the most significant value that we see in Michelle's female leadership qualities is her overwhelming concern for supporting others. Despite her financial success in her first job following law school at Sidley Austin, she was content to take a significant pay cut to pursue her greater passion of serving the community.

This is not to say, however, that she took a pay cut in her overall career. By 2006, according to her tax returns, she earned $273,618 from her role at the University of Chicago Hospitals, which turned out to be significantly more than her husband's income at the time: $157,082 from his position in the U.S. Senate.

While she was initially criticized by close friends when taking a pay cut of more than $40,000 after leaving the law firm despite her significant student debt, Michelle used her intuition and strong sense of self to guide her during these formative years in her career. Concerning yourself with the needs of the community around you by no means has to result in a pay cut for your overall career; by following her true passion and intuition, Michelle was able to make a career out of something that she truly felt driven to do.

4. A CAUTIOUS AND THOUGHTFUL ENTRY INTO POLITICAL LIFE: OBAMA'S CAMPAIGN AND PRESIDENCY

Michelle Obama's inspiring attitude towards her husband's political career is one of the things that ultimately sets her apart as a forward-thinking, strong, independent First Lady. It was clear that the couple did not take Barack's decision to enter into political life lightly, and made cautious, conscious decisions when it came to the future of their family life. Through her intelligence and negotiation skills, Michelle was able to mold her and her husband's position in the spotlight into the best thing for her, her husband, and her family. This chapter will focus on the takeaways from this time in her life and the methods that readers can employ to exercise leadership in their family and take control of their lives.

4.1 Becoming a Mother: The Birth of Two Daughters

When the Obama's daughters Malia and Sasha were born in 1998 and 2001, the couple's priorities shifted, and Michelle's primary focus became the well-being of her daughters. Even after Obama was elected to the senate, the family chose to remain in Chicago's South Side: community was important, especially to Michelle. They preferred the tight-knit nature of their neighborhood to a move to Washington, D.C.

Michelle found a way to prioritize her daughters while continuing to pursue her career at the University of Chicago. In fact, she continued to work part time throughout the girls' childhood. It was only in 2007 that Michelle began to scale back her professional obligations to help balance her family values with Barack's campaign.

The couple devised a thoughtful strategy during the campaign: Michelle's mother, Marian, would care for the girls while Michelle and Barack were out campaigning, but they committed to only being out of the house overnight once per week, which meant campaigning during the day and returning home to their girls before the end of the second day.

This intentional parenting is reflective of how much value Michelle put into what she had learned from her own childhood, and how much she recognized the importance of having her parents playing a daily role in her upbringing. Her father, despite being sick for much of her childhood, had rarely missed a day of work, yet she learned from his sacrifice and recognized what he was doing for his family and strove to follow his example.

4.2 Defining Priorities

Michelle's support for Barack's campaign was thoughtful and not without careful consideration. She sought to be a role model first for her daughters, and then for girls and underrepresented populations all over the country and the world.

A Newsweek article from just before the inauguration reported what a friend said of the girls when they were about to move into the White House: "They're not anxious. They're excited. There's a good anticipation.' It's Michelle who has questions and concerns. She has sought advice from Hillary Clinton (who counseled her on protecting the kids' privacy) and Rosalynn Carter.

Another friend reported that Michelle's goal was "to raise daughters in the national spotlight...to keep them out of it as much as possible and keep them as normal as possible." Michelle's mother Marian even moved into the White House to keep family close and to help care for the two young girls.

4.3 From "Least Famous Spouse" to First Lady

Early on in Barack's presidential campaign, Michelle was described as the "least famous spouse of all of the democratic front runners" by an MSN article. While Elizabeth Edwards and Bill Clinton were spouses of other democratic candidates, Michelle was relatively unknown in the political world. However, she made it very clear that her role in the campaign was not driven by her own political interests or desire to be involved in the political world, but rather by her allegiance to her husband. She said "My job is not a senior adviser...I am here as a wife."

Some criticized Michelle's sense of humor throughout the campaign, noting that here comments that Barack is simply "a mere mortal" implied that many thought he had the status of a god. Others touched on her race, describing her as an "angry black woman," unfairly attacking her for both her race and her gender.

However, while she soon toned down her sarcasm and her image as first lady evolved greatly from those first moments of campaign fame, she wouldn't allow herself to be silenced. She speaks to the challenges of being the first African-American First Lady:

"Barack and I have been in the public eye for many years now, and we've developed a thick skin along the way. When you're out campaigning, there will always be criticism. I just take it in stride and at the end of the day, I know that it comes with the territory."

4.4 Caution and Intuition on the Road to Leadership: Lessons from a Grounded First Lady

The important takeaways from this chaotic time in Michelle's life are her admirable attitude of calm and focus. She followed her intuition and heeded her sense of caution, which allowed her and her family to enter the White House with a very firm sense of their values.

5. THE EVOLUTION OF THE FIRST LADY

5.1 Family First: Leading Two Young Daughters

As mentioned in the last chapter, Michelle had a very deliberate attitude toward her daughters' upbringing.

In a comment about not often including the girls in large events, she responded that "We generally don't include the girls. We try to normalize their lives as much as possible...a lot of this stuff we do, they're like regular kids -- they're running in the opposite direction of what we do."

As much as she tries to normalize her own daughters' lives, Michelle has taken on a number of causes during her time as First Lady to try and normalize other kids' and families' lives--by instilling the same values of education, healthy, and family that she encourages for her own children.

5.2 Michelle's Causes: From Obesity to Girls Education

The family theme is obvious in its importance throughout all of Michelle's initiatives as First Lady.

The First Lady's first and perhaps most recognized project during her time in the White House is *Let's Move*, which she founded in 2010 with the lofty goal of solving the childhood obesity epidemic within a generation.

Her female perspective allows her to multi-task, adopting a multi-faceted approach toward the serious problem of obesity in the United States. By drawing together a broad community of individuals and organizations, she spearheaded efforts to have healthier food in schools and homes, to encourage physical activity, to support parents, and to combat the junk food industry in favor of nutritious choices.

"Everyone has a role to play in reducing childhood obesity...your involvement is key." This type of inclusive leadership is characteristically a female strength. By drawing on this and using it to her advantage, Michelle has experienced significant success in her campaign. From legislation helping public schools to offer healthier meals to corporate commitments to improve access to nutritious food to partnerships with 157 hospitals for more nutritious foods. This project was a shining example of the power of collaborative leadership.

Michelle's second cause was founded in 2011 with Jill Biden, wife of the Vice President. The two women called for Americans to support service members, veterans, and their families. This initiative "works hand in hand with the public and private sector to ensure that service members, veterans, and their families have the tools they need to succeed throughout their lives." This project serves as another excellent example of a community initiative that seeks to draw strength from people working together.

Reach Higher, Michelle's third project, launched in 2014 with the goal of encouraging young people to complete higher education, regardless of whether it is education through a professional training program, community college, or four-year program at a college or university. Through Reach Higher, Michelle seeks to expose students to academic and financial resources they need to support them in their continuing education.

This project is perhaps the most personal to the First Lady's own experience. Recalling the lack of support she received from her high school and her teachers when she aimed to be accepted by Princeton, it is not surprising that she would choose something that aims to give today's students the experience she would have wanted when considering her high aspirations.

Michelle's most recent initiative, entitled Let Girls Learn, is a collaboration with President Obama. It focuses on educating and empowering girls internationally to focus on their education. It aims to raise awareness of educational opportunities in other countries so that girls are both allowed and encouraged to commit to their education. This is the project--once Malia and Sasha are settled in their new post-White House home, of course--that Michelle plans to focus on once Barack's term ends.

5.3 Criticism

From the moment Michelle started campaigning for her husband, she has received much criticism targeted at her race and gender. Described many times as an "angry black woman" during the campaign, Michelle doesn't let critics get away with their blatant racism and sexism.

As she reflected on the campaign trail, she commented on all of the extra considerations that came with being the first African-American first lady. "As potentially the first African-American first lady, I was also the focus of another set of questions and speculations, conversations sometimes rooted in the fears and misperceptions of others…was I too loud or too angry or too emasculating? Or was I too soft, too much a mom, not enough of a career woman?" Michelle, made a good point in mentioning the added criticisms of visible female leaders that are also mothers. She constantly faces criticism of spending too much time and energy being a mother, or too little.

A 2013 article in Politico Magazine named Michelle "a feminist nightmare," stating that her activities as First Lady put too much focus on exercise habits and healthy eating, and motherhood, and not enough on serious policy issues, especially those that concern gender equality. The article states, "she is one of the most influential black women on the planet, and I consider it a national shame that she's not putting the weight of her office behind some of these issues."

In a 2015 commencement speech to graduates at Tuskegee University, Michelle addressed the audience at the historically black university by facing racist and sexist issues head-on. She raised the issue of her family's visibility drawing visible racist attacks. Of her husband, she said that "Even today, there are still folks questioning his citizenship." Many criticized Michelle for this particular speech, and for continuing to fight for the visibility of African-American Issues. A Washington Post article summarized the sentiment of the time: "Right. Blacks have a president now, so they should stop complaining. I hear that argument a lot from conservatives."

In a New Yorker cover cartoon, Michelle appeared, illustrated with a big Afro and a machine gun. She says that moment "knocked me back a bit" and "it made me wonder, just how are people seeing me?" Michelle makes many people, especially conservatives, uncomfortable because she pushes back, she questions things, and she uses her female leadership strengths to her advantage.

But despite all the criticism, Michelle pushes on with her characteristic positivity and perseverance. Her strength lies in her ability to see all of the problems facing her, but at the same time push through them. It seems that she has finally found her stride. She continues to be true to the issues that have been important to her all along. Peter Slevin adds in his biography of Michelle, that "She has found her voice in talking particularly about inequality and the lack of fairness in society, and she has returned to a role that has been important to her since she was a young woman, as a mentor,"

Perhaps the biggest takeaway from this period in Michelle's time as First Lady is her focus on improvement as a community, and not leaving anyone behind. Through her community initiatives, she has gained so much recognition. In her words, "Our history... teaches us that when we pull ourselves out of those lowest emotional depths, and we channel our frustrations into studying and organizing and banding together ... we can take on those deep-rooted problems, and together — together — we can overcome anything that stands in our way." Continuing to draw on her strong values of community, Michelle pushes forward.

5.4 Moving Forward: Beyond the White House

Following the end of her husband's second term, Michelle looks forward to normal life. She has commented that one of the first things she would like to do once Barack's term ends is "open a window," as well as other little things, like going to Target on her own. Given her background, it's no surprise that Michelle wants to be more independent.

In terms of her projects though, Michelle says ""We really want to have some movement on girls' education," she said of her and Barack. "This is the kind of work Barack and I want to do after we leave the White House."

"Our goal is to make sure every girl on the planet gets the opportunity that our girls get."

6. LEADING IN STYLE: PUBLIC IMAGE AND POPULAR CULTURE

In popular culture, Michelle Obama is recognized for her economically accessible style, her enviably toned arms, and her identification as a role model internationally.

However, Michelle's image means much more than simply the labels that she chooses and the dresses she dons for state dinners. Both her clothing style, as well as her leadership style have gained her respect from women and men alike from all over the world. This chapter will examine her broader image as a First Lady and the global perspective of her as a leader. Finally, we will look at her contributions to society during her time as First Lady and compare them to past First Ladies.

6.1 More than Classic Clothes

"What you wear is essentially who you are," Michelle has said of her view on fashion. She encourages women to choose clothes that make them feel comfortable and happy in their own skin.

Her style has been described as "fashion populist," referring to her designer taste mixed in with pieces from, most notably, J.Crew and Target, which have both benefited greatly from her endorsement.

After meeting the Queen of England wearing her elegant dress by designer Isabel Toledo, the Chicago

Tribune reported that "First Lady Michelle Obama showcased her versatility and officially became one of the fab four of the political fashion world in the modern era—joining Jacqueline Kennedy, French first lady Carla Bruni-Sarkozy and Princess Diana."

Adding to the buzz about her clothes, which grab attention for being iconic and having the perfect balance of class and style, Michelle's biceps have earned a fair share of press. *New York Times* columnist commented that Michelle's arms, in her sleeveless State Dinner dress, were the "only bracing symbol of American strength right now".

Some might argue that Michelle's style and public image conform to the "feminist nightmare" persona that some have assigned to her. However, her commitment to displaying more affordable (than the typical designer wardrobes that First Ladies of the past have donned) is unique. But why can't a First Lady be celebrated for her fashion choices and her career accomplishments at the same time? Leading by example, Michelle's simultaneous embrace of fashion and policy serves as an inspiration for women young and old.

6.2 Awards and Accomplishments

Michelle has earned a range of awards and recognition for her accomplishments as First Lady. She was the first sitting First Lady to tweet on Twitter, which adds to her social media portfolio. This distinction of first tweeting First Lady contributes to the populist feel of Michelle's leadership. Through her various social media outlets, she attempts to give the public a view into her life and allow them to feel involved in her causes and share her values.

In recognition of her causes related to children, she earned the Kid's Choice Big Help Award in 2010, and the Shorty Special Award for GIFStar in 2013.

Despite a large calling for her to run for president, Michelle has confirmed that that is not at all in her plans. Yet, without any intention to run, she received 22% in presidential polls in May 2015, higher than any other democratic candidate besides Hillary Clinton, a testament to her leadership pull.

In the sphere of popular culture, Michelle has earned a significant amount of recognition. She was named in *Essence* magazine's "25 of the World's Most Inspiring Women" and in the *Vanity Fair* list of top 10 best dressed list. She became the first First Lady to present an Oscar at the Academy Award in 2013 (to the movie *Argo*).

One of the largest criticisms of Michelle centers around the contrast between her high level of education and her relatively low level of political involvement, while many celebrate her embrace of fashion and lifestyle issues. The often-contrasting comparisons to First Ladies of the past underline this clash in public opinion.

6.3 Comparisons to Past First Ladies

Despite the criticism that Michelle has focused more on lifestyle initiatives than on real policy issues, others have defended her, saying that she could not have taken on policy issues earlier on in her husband's presidency because she would have faced significant resistance. Says Catherine Allgor, history professor at the University of California Riverside, and author of multiple books about first ladies, "Just look at the reaction to her suggestions that people eat salad," referring to the resistance of her efforts to fight childhood obesity.

Many have compared Michelle to Jacqueline Kennedy for her sense of style and class, although a Newsweek article criticizes this comparison, noting that Kennedy gave up her promising writing career when she married John F. Kennedy as a senator. By comparing Michelle to Kennedy, the article states that it risks limiting her to just her style, when her career amounts to so much more.

More recently, Michelle has been compared to Barbara Bush for her discipline and higher education (only she, Bush, and Clinton have graduate degrees).

Many have said that she takes on the all-too-expected role of the woman of the house, dedicating herself to projects including gardening, exercising, and healthy eating. However, while the headlines of the moment focus on Michelle's latest event gown, historians reportedly say that she will eventually be known for her causes and contributions to society.

6.4 Lead like a Female, Lead like Michelle

Michelle Obama's embrace of causes traditionally ascribed to females conforming to traditional gender roles--gardening, exercise, healthy eating--has earned her significant criticism from the feminist community in general. However, her use of leadership qualities characteristic to female leaders has made her a role model in this same field.

Consider the qualities that we have examined throughout this book: following intuition, sticking together, emotional intelligence, and giving to others. Now examine your life for ways that you can incorporate them to improve your leadership skills, regardless of your gender.

THE END

Made in the USA
Middletown, DE
24 July 2017